W9-CLD-383

Written by Dr. Jennifer Bennett

Illustrated & designed by Ailsa Hutton

For Clint
The Daddy I dreamed my children would have. – J.B.

This is River.

Our family!

River lives with her mommy, daddy, and 2 **cats** named Salt and Pepper. 🐾🐾

Do you have any pets like River does? 🐾🐾

One day, River became CURIOUS about how she was born. She knew that she came from her Mommy's **belly**, but how did she ever get in there?

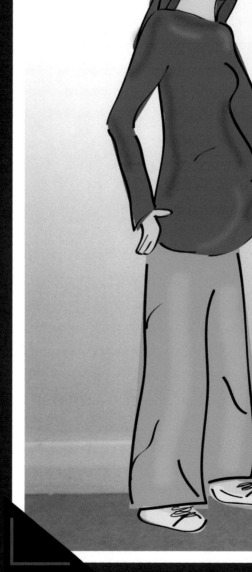

Due day

So River asked her mommy and daddy, **Where did I come from?**

They replied... You were created through a mixture of

SCIENCE

and

love.

You are our...

Mommy continued,

Before you were born, Daddy and I **DREAMED** of sharing our life with a little girl or little BOY.
We wanted Mommy to become pregnant so we could have a baby,

Daddy said.

All babies come from a woman who is pregnant. The baby **grows** inside the woman until the WONDERFUL DAY when the baby is born.

Have you ever seen a pregnant woman?

Most women
become pregnant
by making *love*
with a man,
said Mommy.

Making *love*
happens when
grown-ups get
close in a
special way.

Inside, men have tiny sperm that are like seeds.

They are so *tiny* that you can only see them with a microscope.

Have you ever used **a** microscope?

Inside, all women have very tiny ova which we call eggs. If the sperm and egg meet inside of the woman's body then the woman becomes pregnant!

So how did I grOW inside Mommy's belly?

River wanted to know.

You see, Daddy continued,
time passed and
Mommy didn't become pregnant.
So we decided to see a special doctor
named Dr. Gary.

Do you know your doctor's name?

Dr. Gary was so friendly. He explained that many people need help from a doctor to become pregnant. He examined Mommy and Daddy and discovered that the eggs inside Mommy needed help getting to meet the sperm from Daddy.

The doctor prescribed special medicine to make this happen.

Miracle medicine!

Exclaimed River.

Mommy took the *medicine!* everyday by injection. Daddy helped me, said Mommy.
Even though this was a little painful we hoped it would help me to become pregnant.

This is what we wanted more than **anything!**

Have you ever wanted anything so much?

Then came the very
SPECIAL DAY when we
would have 'IN VITRO FERTILIZATION'
It's a very big word so we just call
it IVF, explained Mommy.

Right, Daddy said, IVF is when the doctor takes the man's sperm
and the woman's eggs and puts them together inside the woman's
body. This can make a woman pregnant, but it doesn't always work.

After the IVF Mommy was told to rest at home and wait. It would take two whole weeks to find out if she became pregnant from the IVF.

Have you ever had to wait and wait for something you wanted so badly?

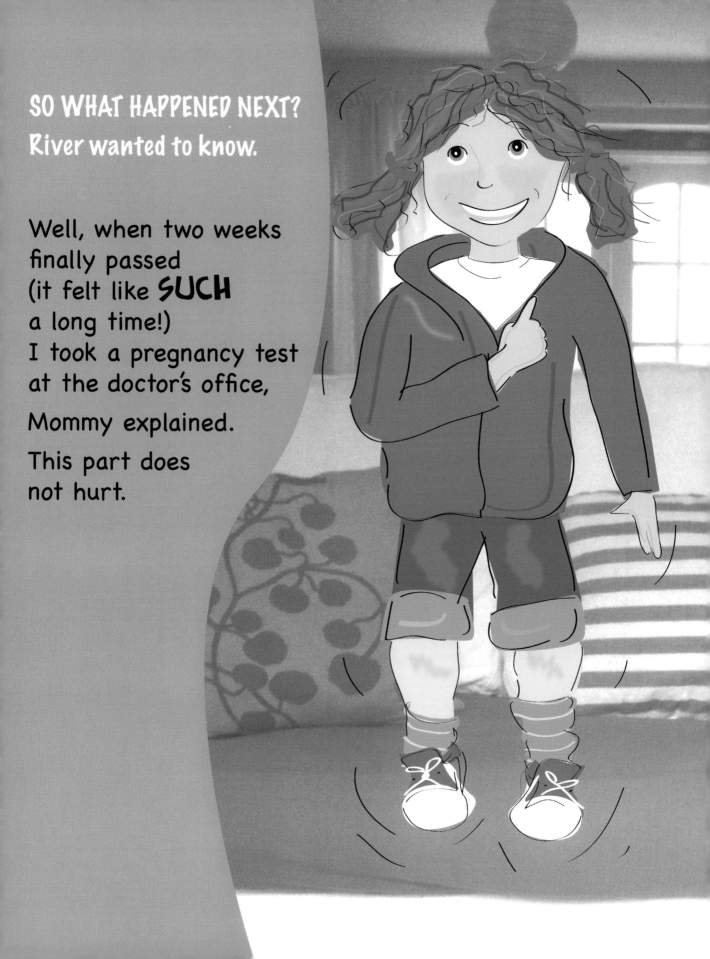

SO WHAT HAPPENED NEXT?
River wanted to know.

Well, when two weeks
finally passed
(it felt like **SUCH**
a long time!)
I took a pregnancy test
at the doctor's office,

Mommy explained.

This part does
not hurt.

Nurse Jane said we would have the test results soon. More waiting! But two hours later, Nurse Jane called with terrific news.

THE IVF WORKED!

WE WERE GOING TO HAVE A BABY!

THAT WAS ME! Cheered River.

Daddy told River, Mommy's belly became bigg**er** and BIGGER over the next nine months as you were growing inside of her.

Have you ever touched the belly of a pregnant woman?

You were born in the
very early morning
on July first,
said Mommy.

It was a
WONDERFUL
DAY to meet
our..........

River comes home!

Jennifer Bennett, Psy.D. is a doctor of clinical psychology with a focus on children and families. She lives in Santa Monica, California with her wonderful husband, two incredible daughters and two very entertaining cats.

www.drjennybennett.com
drjennyb@mac.com

Ailsa Hutton is a Scottish illustrator and designer. She studied illustration at Edinburgh's Telford College. At 23 years old she is looking forward to a long and exciting career illustrating/designing and traveling the world.
info@thecuillincollective.co.uk

Coming soon- Ruby's Arrival - A new baby is coming, but River isn't sure she wants to become a big sister.

LaVergne, TN USA
27 June 2010
187534LV00002B